Children Grieve Too:

a handbook for parents of grieving children and teens

Table of Contents

Introduction — 1

Chapter 1: Breaking the News — 2

Chapter 2: Involving your children in mourning rituals — 5

Chapter 3: Now what? Looking at grief from a developmental perspective — 9

Chapter 4: What is this thing called Grief? — 17

Chapter 5: Where is my Dad now? What happens after death? — 23

Chapter 6: Sibling Grief — 25

Chapter 7: How can I help my children? — 28

Chapter 8: Assemble your team — 32

Chapter 9: Help your children maintain the connection and memorialize their loved one — 36

Chapter 10: Frequently asked questions — 39

Chapter 11: Helping Your Child Cope with Your New Relationship — 44

Chapter 12: There's no such thing as Closure! — 46

INTRODUCTION

The unimaginable has happened. Your spouse or partner has died and you are faced with the daunting task of parenting your grieving children alone. Or you were divorced and co-parenting when the death of your former spouse occurred, leaving you a single parent for the first time. Perhaps you have experienced the death of one of your children and you are coping with not only your own unbearable grief but also the grief of your surviving children. Either way, it is hard to be hopeful that you and your family will find a way to survive and that it won't always feel this bad.

During the past 20 years grief specialists have done their best to provide parents with guidelines that would make the enormous task of parenting their grieving children feel more manageable. But children's grief, like adult grief, doesn't fit into neat stages with easy 'fixes'. Instead, the grief process is a unique experience for each and every child, teen, or adult. You can, however, establish yourself as the Captain of a team of compassionate and skilled people who can help you through the challenging first years in your mourning process. Only the passage of time will convince you that, as the Captain, all of you will not only survive but can actually thrive!

By virtue of the fact that you are choosing to read this book, you are taking a positive step in the right direction. Consumed with your own grief, it's hard enough to manage the tasks of day to day life let alone find time to read. This book is designed to provide basic information that will greatly contribute to a successful outcome for you and your children while not requiring hours and hours of uninterrupted reading time.

CHAPTER 1: BREAKING THE NEWS

While your children may consider themselves 'all grown up,' they are in fact still developing physically, cognitively and emotionally well into their 20's. It is important that you use age-appropriate language when speaking to your children about death. Be mindful of the fact that children cannot tolerate intense emotions or focus their attention for as long as you can.

Experts agree that you should always be honest with your child when a death is anticipated or has occurred. In some cases there is the opportunity to prepare your child for the probability that your loved one's life is coming to an end. Taking the time to talk with them will help them understand what is happening. Even so, as long as the person is still breathing, your children will most likely maintain hope that their loved one will survive. In spite of your best efforts, no matter how well you have readied your child, it will still be a shock when the death actually occurs. As one child put it:

*"I didn't know he was going to die **that** night."*

It is essential to your child's grieving process that you explain what is happening to their loved one in simple, direct, age appropriate language. As death is the ultimate and last taboo subject in our dominant culture, euphemisms are often used in an attempt to shield grievers from the full impact of the realization that a death has occurred. While adults understand the meaning behind the most common euphemisms for death, they can be confusing to children.

The most widely used euphemisms for death include saying someone *"passed away"*, *"passed"*, or that we *"lost"* him or her.

Religious euphemisms may be comforting to some adults but don't comfort children in the same way. For example when people say *"God took your sister because she was so good"* a child might worry that God would take other *"good"* family members or might decide she better NOT be good or God might take her too!

After a protracted and painful dying process adults may be comforted by the knowledge that their loved one is no longer suffering. Caring adults may say to children that *"father is in a better place"* or that *"Grandma is with God now"* but as one child said:

"I don't care that dad is with God, I want him at my soccer game!"

Euphemistic sayings like these or 'he's gone to heaven' impinge on the child's ability to understand what has happened to their loved one. Instead, saying the person is **dead** or **died** helps your children begin to understand and accept the reality of what has actually occurred.

Many of the sleep disturbances which arise after a death do so because a well meaning adult has told a child that their loved one '*is sleeping.*' When the child realizes that the loved one is no longer there for them, they may be reluctant to fall asleep or sleep apart from you for fear that they or another family member will disappear.

Similarly, people don't die because they are "sick." They die due to a specific medical problem, an accident, or other cause. Children who are told that someone died because they were sick will be fearful when he or other loved ones get sick. Instead, offer simple, age appropriate explanations such as:

"The doctors tried lots of medicines and treatments to help daddy get better but there wasn't any medicine that would make daddy's cancer go away and his body stopped working and he died."

For children under age 7 or 8 you will need to explain what 'dead' means. You can help them understand that:

"When someone dies they can no longer hear, move, see or smell and we will never see them alive again."

In the event of a sudden death such as a car accident, natural disaster, heart attack, homicide, overdose or suicide it is equally important to be truthful. Children eventually find out the truth and if you haven't been honest with them they will feel angry and have difficulty trusting you and others in the future.

Start simply and then add more details in response to their questions. Consider the way you taught them 'where babies come from' and use that as a guide. If they don't want details yet tell them "when you are ready to hear more I will tell you." For example:

"Your brother was crossing the street and a car hit him. His body was injured so badly that the paramedics and doctors could not fix him and he died." Or, *"mom was at work and a bad man with a gun shot her and she died."*

If your loved one died suddenly from a heart attack offer a similar explanation:

"Mommy's heart wasn't working properly and it stopped beating and she died."

Remember, the language you use when talking to your children about the death will signal to them that you are available to have that conversation and that they can come to you for both comfort and information.

CHAPTER 2:
INVOLVING YOUR CHILDREN IN MOURNING RITUALS

Grievers of all ages may benefit from taking an active role in the funerary process. Some family members lovingly wash and dress the deceased and lay the body out in the family home on a bed or 'wake table.' Family members can choose to build caskets and design head stones and cook or bake for the guests who will attend the viewing, wake or service. These are among the last acts of love and kindness you can perform for your person who died.

Many clergy include children in planning the mourning ceremonies and rituals and offer suggestions as to ways children can participate. One child who attended the funeral later proudly reported:

"I helped carry the casket with father's friends."

Children can also sing a song, pick out the clothing or place treasured items in the casket along with the body.

Some cultures or families are reluctant to involve their children in mourning rituals for fear that it will frighten them and detract from their positive memories of the person before the death. Until recently it was common not to include children when preparations for mourning rituals were being made. Children were often not even invited or expected to participate during the funeral, memorial service, or a celebration of life.

Current understandings of grief suggest that children derive the same benefits that adults do when they participate in mourning rituals. The comfort and support provided by family and friends in the first weeks after the death help buoy their spirits and provide a buffer to the intensity of feelings that will eventually surface. Attendance at funerary rituals helps because the rituals provide structure as everyone begins the mourning process. Attendance at viewings, mass, services or memorials also helps the children begin to understand and cope with the reality of the death. For example, a viewing offers the attendees the opportunity to see that the person in the casket is, without a doubt, their loved one. Consider this as a chance for you and your children to see the body of the person who died one the last time and say "good-bye."

Most importantly, after a death, children need to remain in close proximity to those adults they love most both for comfort and to alleviate fears of further abandonment. A thorough explanation by caring adults prepares them for what will take place during the mourning ritual and may ameliorate their shock and distress. Older relatives, not familiar with more modern thinking, might try to discourage you from including the children. Young family members who are excluded due to cultural or familial beliefs often express anger once they learn that other children had the chance to participate.

When preparing your children for mourning rituals, give them information about what to expect. For example, tell them who will be there, how those people might be acting, and where you and the children will be seated. Designate another adult who hasn't been impacted as directly by the death as you have to companion your child. Be sure and let the children know they can take a break and go outside if they need to.

For very young children you can start the conversation by saying:

"Grandma and I and all the other grownups we love are going to go say good-bye to Daddy and we'd like you to join us. Many other people will be there who cared about Daddy. The priest (rabbi or minister) *will lead some prayers and some people will get up and say nice things about Daddy. You can say something too if you'd like."*

Your child may be too numb to remember details about the day but will later be glad they were part of the rituals and had the opportunity to say good-bye and show their respects along with other family members.

If there will be a viewing or open casket funeral you and your children may experience shock at the way the person who died looks. Adequate preparation will lessen the negative impact of the sight of the deceased. This image, if disturbing, will typically recede over time while memories from when the person was alive will remain.

If there will be a viewing, explain:

"We will get to see Daddy's body but it might look different. His eyes will be closed and he won't be moving or looking at us and he won't be able to talk to us because he isn't alive anymore. If you'd like, you can bring something to put in the casket that will be with his body when the casket is buried in the ground."

In addition you may want to add:

"He may feel cold or different than when he was alive if you touch him" or as one child put it after viewing her mother's body:

"She felt like a doll."

Also let them know that the person's hair and makeup may be styled differently than when they were alive.

For a closed casket service, tell the children:

"We won't get to see Daddy because his body will be in a long box called a casket but we can still say good-bye to him out loud or in our minds."

Provide additional information about who will be attending and how people might act. For example:

"Some people may feel like crying and that is natural but it's also okay not to cry. If you need to go outside for a break your Aunt Caroline will take you and you can come back when you feel ready."

End the conversation by asking the child if they have any questions.

If you decide not to include your children, or if the ritual has already occurred you can invite them to visit the location of the burial site or scattering at a later time. You can offer to tell them about the service that took place including who was present, who spoke, what was said, answering additional questions as they arise.

Prior to future visits to the cemetery, invite your children to accompany you by saying:

"I'm going to visit Mommy's grave at the cemetery. Would you like to go too?"

While some children prefer not to go with you, others enjoy bringing flowers, balloons, painted rocks or other handmade objects when they visit the gravesite. If you invite them in a non-threatening manner most children will want to go with you. If he or she refuses never force them. Ask them to let you know when they are ready to go and continue to invite them until that day arrives.

Alternately, children can create their own memorial space in their room where they can go to honor the memory of their loved one. Similar to a shrine, they can place photos and other items that remind them of their person who died and they can spend time there at their leisure.

CHAPTER 3:
NOW WHAT? LOOKING AT GRIEF FROM A DEVELOPMENTAL PERSPECTIVE

It may be days, even weeks before helpful friends and relatives return to their own routines and you and your children begin to experience your new life without your loved one who died. The way you and the children operate during the first weeks after the death will set the stage for the future. Though it may be hard to find the strength, establish yourself as the leader of the family while respecting the children's roles and individuality. Create an atmosphere for supporting one another when the inevitable waves of grief wash over you. At the same time, model for your children that, in spite of your grief, life continues, and it's okay to take breaks and engage in social and other life enhancing activities.

Adults are often unprepared for the big difference between how their children grieve and the way that adults express their grief. Parents are surprised when their children do not talk to them about the person who died or go to them for comfort and support.

 Well-meaning friends and family may have told your children that they *"need to look after their mother"*, *"be the man of the house"* or *"help dad with little ones now that mom is gone."*

In some cases the person who is dying may ask the child to look after mother, father or the other children in the family. Even if no one has actually said this to your children, they may feel as if they must assume adult responsibilities or keep their feelings to themselves in an effort to protect you, their surviving parent, from being overwhelmed.

These external or internal cues may interfere with your children's developmental imperative to begin the separation individuation process. In spite of the death, all children need the chance to begin to experience themselves in relation to others outside the family as well as to participate in the same age-appropriate activities as their non-bereaved peers.

Be mindful of the fact that as your child moves through different developmental stages they may experience unfamiliar cognitive or emotional grief reactions. Reassure them that this is a normal part of growing up and that their grief will continue to change as they grow older.

DEVELOPMENTAL STAGES AND CHILDREN'S RESPONSES TO GRIEF
0-2 yrs: Irritability, changes in sleeping, eating, and toilet habits, fear of abandonment, regression to previous level of functioning, react to absence of the deceased attachment figure and to responses of the adults around him
2-5 yrs: Confusion, separation anxiety, withdrawn behavior or depressed affect, nightmares, regression, fear that someone else will soon die too
5-8 yrs: Confusion, anger, denial of the reality, repeated questioning about the cause of the death and what happens to the body, excess energy, somatic complaints
8-12 yrs: Morbid curiosity about death or fear of death, difficulty concentrating
Teens: Denial, anxiety, anger, depression, trouble concentrating, academic problems, isolating, persistent anger or sadness, somatic complaints, poor judgment/impulsive behavior, shifting moods, disturbance in separation and individuation

Developmental differences

a. Pre-school aged children (2-5 years) – don't understand death related concepts. They don't know that death is irreversible and permanent and may fully expect the person to reappear like other things that go away and come back. They can't understand non-functionality, or that the body stops working and that the person can no longer see, feel, hear, taste or smell. Magical in their thinking, they believe that they can 'wish their person back to life' or convince themselves that their absence is only temporary.

Pre-school aged children are also ego-centric and believe that they are at the center of the events happening around them. They are likely to think that they caused the death of their loved one and feel guilty. Telling them *'it's not your fault'* won't take the guilty feeling away but pointing out the misperceptions in their thinking can help. For example, if your pre- school aged child thinks they caused the death because they spilled their milk, remind them of all the other times they spilled their milk and no one died. Tell them that:

"making someone angry doesn't cause them to die. People die because they were in a car accident." (Or insert a description of what caused your loved one to die)

Since the pre-school aged child lacks the verbal skills of older children they may act out their grief instead of talking about it. They may play 'shoot-em up' games after a homicide, crash their toy cars after a car accident or bury their dolls in the sand box in an effort to gain a sense of mastery over the situation. Anger and frustration may incite the child to break things, strike out or be uncooperative.

Demonstrating that you recognize and understand their feelings will ease their pain. For example try saying:

"I see you keep building with legos and then knocking them down. That is a good way to let the anger out that you feel because Daddy died."

Although your pre-school aged child has adjusted to life at day care or school they may regress back to the time when any separation from you caused extreme anxiety. When they refuse to get ready for school they are not attempting to manipulate you in order to avoid school but are literally terrified to be separated from you for fear that another death will occur while you are apart.

Experts agree that returning to school and other everyday routines helps your children begin to adjust to their life without their loved one and teaches them that there is still some predictability in life. School and playing with friends offer needed distractions from their grief and an important opportunity for you to have some alone time. On the other hand, an occasional day off from school and work can offer you all a chance to engage in some relaxation or fun time and reduce the day- to-day anxiety you may all experience when separated from one another because of your weekday commitments.

b. Elementary school- aged children (6-11 years) are concrete thinkers and want details to help them make sense of the death. They too may lack the ability to express their feelings verbally and are still learning self control so they may 'act out' their grief in destructive ways. Children of this age may not be ready to tolerate strong emotion for very long and may prefer not to talk or even think about their loved one who died.

The amount of details you offer when describing how your special person died should vary from child to child. Be prepared to offer more information when your children ask for it. The children will revisit their grief when they reach other developmental stages or milestones so be prepared to repeat or add more information to your explanation all over again.

Like pre-school aged children, intense fears of someone else dying or leaving may catapult them into your bed at night.   They feel less safe at night, especially if their father has died, and generally fear that they or someone else might die while they are sleeping. Children who have slept in their own beds for years may want to sleep near you to soothe their fears. If your children are concerned that they might die, offer reassurance that you can't "catch" death. Most importantly tell them that:

"most people live until they are very, very old."

Without the distractions of the day your children may also feel the pain of the loss more at night. Bed time rituals may have been disrupted by the death. Bed time may be the only time your child is alone all day. Most children report that they cry and feel lonely most often at night.

Help their school personnel understand that separations are difficult and ask them to allow your children to phone you when they feel the need to know you are safe. They may also need proximity to you after school or on weekends for comfort and may isolate from their peers, choosing instead to stay home with you where they can "make sure" that nothing bad happens.

Your children may talk about dying or say they wish they were dead. Usually this is because they would like to be reunited with the person who died or see him or her one more time. In other cases this may be indicative of a more serious depression or suicidality. Seek professional help if your children are preoccupied with thoughts of their own death. Even very young children are capable of ending their own life because they don't understand the consequences of their actions (see Chapter 10).

c. Teens- (12-18 years) Though your teens may try and tell you that they are your equal, their brains are still forming. Recent studies show that the human brain continues to grow until age 25. Your teen's grief process is different from that of adults because they are developmentally younger, both cognitively and emotionally. Teens, like pre-school aged children, can be ego-centric thinkers. They too think that the world revolves around them and are therefore likely to think that they have somehow caused the death of their loved one. The feelings of guilt that accompany this type of thinking can be acutely painful and if your teens are convinced the death was their fault, no amount of reassurance from you will alter that perception. Time will help ease the pain but therapy may be advisable when guilt is the dominate grief-related feeling.

Because their brains are still developing, teens are likely to make decisions that you wouldn't agree with and would consider unwise or impulsive. Teens may also engage in practices which are self-destructive in an effort to distract themselves from and cope with their grief.

Your teens may define themselves by their relationship to others. It is critically important to them that they fit in with their desired peer group. Differences between themselves and their peers at this age can be devastating. It is not uncommon for teens to keep their grief to themselves choosing for example to tell their peers that their father is "on a business trip" rather than saying that their father "died" and being noticeably different.

Like their younger siblings, they do not have the emotional capacity to withstand intense emotion for very long. They need time to be 'a kid' and should not be expected to assume too many adult-like responsibilities. Grieving teens are even more likely than their peers to be expected to assume adult roles prematurely or may take on more responsibility themselves out of filial loyalty. This will impact their ability to grieve the death and may interfere with the developmental imperative to separate and individuate from the family.

Some teens might be better able to hide their grief so they don't receive the attention that their younger sibs or visibly grieving parent receive. Your teen may fall through the cracks as people tend to the adults and younger children in the family.

Regardless of the age or developmental stage of your children at the time of the death the single most important factor impacting their adjustment to the loss will depend on you. Grief experts have found that the way a surviving parent adjusts to the loss of their spouse or child directly impacts the outcome of the mourning process for their children. The sooner you get the support you need to parent your grieving children and get support for your own grief, the better your child will adapt to the loss.

CHAPTER 4:
WHAT IS THIS THING CALLED GRIEF?

People typically use the word "grief" to describe the feeling of sadness that most mourners experience. Grief is more than sadness. Grief is the internal response of the mourner including all the feelings and thoughts that a person experiences when someone they care about dies.

In the immediate aftermath of the death, human beings are protected from experiencing overly intense emotions by way of a process referred to as 'psychic numbing.' Grievers report feeling numb or that they feel as if they have a protective cocoon around them. Children often report feeling 'nothing' or that they feel 'fine' for lack of a more articulate way to explain the numbness.

Your children may not look like they are grieving because they ran off to play shortly after you told them about the death. When this happens, your children are merely taking a break from grief because it is hard for children to withstand intense emotions. Play, school, or homework provide a needed distraction or break and reassures them that there is still some order and predictability in the world. They will eventually return to their grief when they are ready.

Be mindful that your children aren't distracting themselves in ways that are harmful to themselves or others. As children's brains aren't fully developed it may be hard for them to make good decisions. Your son or daughter may use poor judgment or engage in impulsive or self-destructive behaviors. Even children in primary school are at greater risk for these types of behaviors in the first three years after the death than their non-bereaved peers.

Your child may experience many of the same feelings as you but may not know how to describe the feeling in words.

They also don't understand that we may experience our feelings physically in our bodies. Their stomachache or headache, like yours, may be related to their grief.

Childhood Grief Reactions

Behavioral	Emotional	Social	Cognitive
Hypoactive behavior	Numbness	Overly sensitive	Intrusive images
Hyperactive behavior	Guilt	Dependent	Forgetfulness
Feeling disconnected	Sadness	Withdrawn	Trouble Concentrating
Headaches or stomach aches	Anger	Lack of initiative	Dreams of the deceased
Trouble falling asleep or staying asleep	Fear	Conflicted relationships with peers or siblings	Sense of the love one's presence
Change in appetite	Irritability		Searching for the deceased
Change in weight	Relief or happiness		Nightmares
Fatigue	Longing for the deceased		
self-destructive acts	Anxiety		
Crying	Depression		
Shortness of breath	Apathy		
Constriction of the throat	Loneliness or feeling of abandonment		

- **Sadness** - is an expected part of any grief process. Sadness comes and goes and may be triggered by a sound, a smell, a taste or by the sight of something they associate with the person who died. If your partner has died your child may feel sad when they see other children with two parents. Children feel their sadness at different times of day or night. After school and in the evening may be the hardest times of day because there are fewer distractions in the home than at school or when they are playing with friends. Children, like adults, associate the sadness with 'the broken heart' or the heartache that grievers describe. Just because your children are sad doesn't mean that they will look sad or that they will cry all the time. Most children report that they only cry when they are alone at night in their room. They fear that if they cry in front of other children they will be called "baby" or "cry-baby."

- **Anger** – There are many causes for anger when someone you love dies. Your children may be angry at the person who died for leaving them. They may be angry at you for surviving or blame you for not preventing the death. They may take their anger out on others or do things that are self destructive for lack of the ability to talk about this feeling.

Your child may be angry at the doctors who didn't save the person who died, or at the perpetrator who caused a car accident or other sudden, violent death. Encourage them to express their anger rather than hold it inside where it can cause them to become depressed, develop headaches or stomachaches.

Offer your child suggestions for ways to express their anger. For example teach a young child to punch a designated pillow rather than hit a wall. Suggest that your child scream into a pillow, draw what anger looks like, or blow their anger into a paper bag and then pop the bag, releasing the anger they feel at that moment.

- **Guilt** – Children, like adults, are likely to think they should have been able to prevent the death. They may go so far as to blame themselves for the death and may feel regret that they didn't spend more time with the person while he or she was alive. They may blame themselves for not stopping their parent from smoking, drinking, using illegal substances. They may also erroneously believe that their anger or their words caused the death. As one 9 year-old girl said:

"If I hadn't told my auntie I hated her she wouldn't have had a heart attack and died."

Children engage in other types of erroneous thinking. For example, an 11 year-old boy felt it was his fault that his father died when the car jack broke, crushing his father who was underneath the car making repairs at that time. Telling your child it is not their fault won't instantly relieve them of the guilt. Try instead to look for the logic in their immature thinking. For example, telling the 8 year-old that the car crash *"wasn't their fault"* won't work as well as pointing out that:

"Eight year -olds don't know how to drive so you would not have been able to drive the car to safety."

- **Happiness/Relief** - There is sometimes cause for happiness or relief when someone dies. Your child may be afraid to express those feelings for fear of reproach. People have a tendency to idealize the dead, especially during the first months after the death, and your child may have gleaned that it is wrong to speak ill of the dead.

Under the following circumstances it is natural to feel happiness or relief. When the person dies after a long, painful illness, the children understand that the person is no longer suffering and may feel happy or relieved. In addition, the family members who cared for the dying are now free to spend more time with the children. As one child also expressed:

"Now I don't have to be so quiet in the house. I can run, and make noise and not worry that I am bothering daddy."

When the person who died was abusive towards the child or other family members there may be tremendous relief, even happiness when that person dies. Give your children permission to talk about, not only what they miss about the person who died, but also what they don't miss. Agree with their statements when you can or validate their feelings. For example:

"I don't miss the way mommy used to yell either" or *"I know it bothered you when daddy used bad words. We can still love him and not like that part of him."*

- **Fear -** Especially after the death of a father, children may feel less safe in the world. After school is potentially a scary time for children who have to walk home from school alone or stay home alone because their sibling or parent has died.

Many of the challenging bedtime or night time behaviors are related to fear that someone else might die during the night or that something 'bad' might happen. Children and teens commonly want to sleep with their parent after the death. Many families choose to sleep in the same room for extended periods of time to alleviate some of the fear. There is probably no chance that the children will always want to sleep with you and you may rest assured that they will eventually return to their own beds!

You may see a reappearance of separation anxiety when you drop them at school or attempt to leave younger children with a baby sitter. Your child may want to stay home from school in an attempt to stand guard or gain a sense of control over their environment which feels so out of control after the death.

Your children may also be fearful that they will forget the person who died. Giving them opportunities to look at photos, listen to voice recordings or view home movies helps them hold on to precious memories of the sounds and sight of the person who died.

After the death of a parent, your children may also fear that you will remarry. Please refer to Chapter 11 for discussion of this concern.

CHAPTER 5:
WHERE IS MY DAD NOW?
WHAT HAPPENS AFTER DEATH?

Death may challenge religious and spiritual beliefs and necessitate the need to share with your children your thoughts about life, death, a higher power and the afterlife. In the event of an untimely or particularly cruel type of death, one's belief in a benevolent God may come into question. Some children may want to know:

"If God is good then how could he take my dad away?"

Death raises these and other questions which you may consider as "unanswerable." When it comes to religious or spiritual concerns, many parents find it helpful to consult with clergy. It is also all right to say that you *"don't have an answer but that you understand their question."* Then remember to validate just how hard it is **not** to know why someone dies young or in a traumatic way.

Your child may never have been taught a concept of the afterlife. It's not too late now to share your thoughts or beliefs with them as your spiritual beliefs may be comforting to the child in the same way they are to you.

The majority of children believe there is a heaven and may have highly detailed ideas of what happens there. Young children ascribe life-like qualities to the deceased. Ask your 5-12 year-old to draw 'where the person is now' and they may likely draw a picture of the person who died engaged in some activity the person enjoyed while alive.

The idea of heaven may or may not be comforting to you or your children. Each member of the family should be free to adopt their own beliefs. After all, none of us really knows for sure what happens after death.

Your child may also struggle if they have been taught that 'only good people go to heaven and that bad people go to hell.' Painful thoughts of the person burning alongside the devil can accompany this type of thinking.

Whether you believe that your loved one is still with you in spirit or not, ask your children whether they ever feel that *"daddy is with them."* If they report that they sometimes sense the presence of the deceased, find out whether they like it when that happens or not. If they are comforted by thoughts that their person who died is still with them, then support that type of thinking.

Some people find comfort in the notion that their parent or sibling is watching over them or as one child put it:

"She is my guardian angel and sees everything that happens to me" or as another said *"He is my fairy God-dad!"*

Others might be uncomfortable with the idea that the deceased can watch them from heaven, particularly if they engage in behavior that the deceased would frown upon.

If your spirituality does not include a notion of heaven you may want to consider offering the following explanation:

"While the body no longer works and Daddy is dead, he can still be with you in your mind when you remember him or in your heart when you feel love for him."

Remember that very young children cannot think abstractly so this conversation may lead them to literally picture the person inside their brain or heart in miniature form! When the child reaches a later stage of cognitive development they will realize that this belief is philosophical or metaphorical rather than literal.

CHAPTER 6:
SIBLING GRIEF

Brothers and sisters are as close as hands and feet.
Vietnamese Proverb

If you are reading this chapter it is most likely because you have experienced the death of a child. The following are some important things to consider when you and your family are grieving this particular loss.

When a child dies, the lives of the surviving children in the family are forever altered. Many experts in the field consider the death of a sibling as the most devastating loss that a child can experience after the death of a parent. After the death of a child, the family's available support system typically rallies around the parents, leaving the siblings to grieve alone.

As a grieving parent, you may be so overwhelmed by your own grief that you aren't emotionally or physically as available to your surviving children. This creates a secondary loss for the children. Not only has their sibling died but also the people who they typically turn to for comfort, support, and guidance are not the same as they were before the death. Even infants perceive the slightest changes in their primary caregivers.

Many sibling relationships are characterized by ambivalence. Due to the magical or ego-centric thinking typical in the toddler years and again in adolescence your other children might actually think that they caused the death of their sibling. For example a 7 year-old boy.

old boy reported that in a fit of jealousy he wished his brother was dead. When his brother later died of leukemia, the 7 year-old believed it was his fault. If this happens acknowledge your child's feeling and respond:

"Your anger didn't kill your brother, Cancer did."

(For more on how to support your child when the child feels responsible for the death see Chapter 4)

Your surviving children may also experience relief that they no longer have to compete for your attention or other family resources with their sibling who died. Especially when the child who died had been ill or suffered a long, painful death, you might not have had as much time for your other children. Give your surviving children permission to enjoy being able to spend more time with you now without feeling guilty. Try saying:

"I enjoy having more time to spend with you Max"

When a loved one dies, children may be confronted for the first time with their own mortality. When a sibling dies they see that even a very young person can die. This may cause fear for their own life along with the fear that another family member may die.

After the death of a sibling there is a shift in the entire identity of the surviving children. If your surviving child defines himself as "the big brother," who are they when the little brother has died? If the "smart one" or the "pretty one" dies how does this change who the surviving child is now? Some children may even attempt to assume personality characteristics and interests of their sibling who died.

You may be pondering how to answer the question *"How many children do you have*?" when one of your children has died. There is no wrong or right way to answer this question. Your response may depend on who is asking the question. Some parents chose to say:

"I had three children but one died."

You and your grieving children may be yearning for the companionship of your child who died.

Your surviving children may have lost their most trusted playmate, protector or mentor.

Even the child who is anticipating the birth of a new sibling mourns the loss of that fantasized relationship when there is a perinatal or stillborn death.

Much like when a parent dies, your surviving children may have to assume new roles in the family, including being protective of you, babysitting younger siblings, doing the chores their sibling used to do, etc. You may also become so protective of your surviving children that their normal developmental progress is impacted. For example, you may not feel comfortable letting your 13 year- old go to the mall without you, even though all his friends are allowed to do so.

The death may impact your teen when applying for college. Your teens may intuit that another loss would be too much for you, and therefore delay or give up plans to move away from home for college.   It is recommended that you encourage your college-bound children to follow through with their plans even if that involves moving away from home. This will ensure that the death of their sibling does not prevent them from achieving goals and moving forward with their own growth. Reassuring them that you will be okay without them and that you want them to follow through with their plans will help ease any feelings of fear or guilt they might experience if they chose to go.

On a positive note, research has shown that those children who survive the death of a sibling may grow in self esteem, and maturity. In time your children may come to value life and family more and you and your children may grow closer in healthy ways.

CHAPTER 7:
HOW CAN I HELP MY CHILDREN?

1. **First and foremost, get support for yourself.** Be there for your children, honor their grief, and take good care of yourself. Your children's adjustment to life without their loved one who died is directly impacted and dependent on your own ability to adapt to the loss, and to be available emotionally and physically to your children.

2. **Be a role model for how people grieve.** Don't be afraid to share your grief with your children. You are their role model for all behavior, including how to express grief in a healthy way. If you always hide your own grief, how will they know that it's ok to grieve? When you mask your feelings, you send a strong signal that it's not ok to grieve openly. Your children will follow your example and hide their grief and be left to grieve alone. As one 6 year-old boy stated when asked "when do you cry," he responded:

   "I cry in my mind."

   When children feel they have to hide their tears it leaves them no choice but to cry alone. Reassure them that:

   "When I cry it's because I miss daddy, and it's OK for you to cry, too."

   You can model that crying is natural and that it eventually ends and you are again available to support them. You can cry together and then get back to the business of life, dinner, homework, and play.

3. **Remember that your children are children and not your life partner or confidant.** Limit the amount of information you share with them so they aren't forced

to take on adult worries prematurely. It is not uncommon for children as young as 3 to feel it is their job to cheer up their grieving parent. We have learned that children who are exposed to adult concerns become preoccupied with these types of worries. In the words of one 5 year-old girl:

"My mom went to London to sell the flat because the stock market crashed."

Others worry that:

"They are going to take our car away."

Instead of confiding in your young children, seek support from adults in your community. Limit what you say about your concerns when talking on the telephone if your children are present. If your children do overhear you discussing financial or other adult matters, reassure them that:

"You don't need to worry. Mommy is strong enough to take care of our family."

4. **Include the children in decisions which impact the mourning process.** This includes: when to give away the clothes, take down the photos, or visit the cemetery. Convey you are still a family although some of the roles have shifted and someone very important has died. Try and eat meals together several nights a week. Eating meals together as a family has been found to have a positive impact on academic achievement as well as on the emotional health of children.

5. **Provide structure and routine, as it helps children feel safer.** Remember that after the death, the world feels out of control and unpredictable. Establishing and maintaining schedules, routines and limits will help your

children regain a sense of the world as a safe place and life as being somewhat predictable. This will help them feel less out of control.

Reassign tasks, with you taking on most of the household responsibilities if the deceased was an adult. Expecting even the young children to take on some age-appropriate responsibilities helps strengthen the family unit. If you aren't sure if a chore is age-appropriate find out what types of chores other children their age are doing.

Though children may complain that they have to help out more around the house, it will also teach them responsibility and other important life lessons. Chores should change as children mature. Be prepared to recognize the range of feelings these activities will bring up. Though they may complain that it's *"not fair"* they may also gain a sense of mastery or pride that they can complete these tasks. Don't be afraid to tell your parentally-bereaved child that their parent who died would be proud of the way they help out around the house.

6. **Practice tolerating your children's grief.** Mourning is a lifelong process.   It is hard as a parent to tolerate your child's pain, especially when you are also in distress. At times you may want to wish it away and say to the children: *"oh, you'll get over it."* This will only cause your children to shut down as it signals that you aren't available to join with them in their grief. Instead, encourage them to share their feelings, thoughts and concerns. If your child approaches you at a time when you can't make yourself available, schedule another time to do this rather than just dismissing them.

Respect when your children don't feel like talking about the person who died or about their feelings. It may not be as natural for them to talk about feelings as it may be for you. Be mindful of the fact that by not talking about their grief they may be trying to shield you from their pain. That's their way of taking care of you.

Even though some children may feel comfortable talking about the person who died or crave physical closeness at night they may avoid conversation about feelings related to the death. Remind yourself that they are struggling too, and let yourself off the hook for not being able to fix it for them!

7. **Teach your children ways they can comfort themselves.** Offering your children ideas about ways to ease their pain when you aren't available will help them in all areas of their life. Many children report that petting, walking or talking to their pet, hitting or screaming into a pillow, writing in a journal, drawing, writing songs or poems or playing sports are ways they can cope with their powerful feelings. Children can also blow their anger away with bubbles, release emotion by popping bubble wrap or blow air into a paper bag and then pop the bag. These techniques might be helpful for you as well!

Don't despair! Just by reading this book you are making your children's well-being a priority. This will directly impact your children's grieving process in a positive way.

CHAPTER 8:
ASSEMBLE YOUR TEAM

As a newly widowed parent or a parent grieving the death of a child, first and foremost recognize that you can't be all things to your children. What you can be is the captain of a team of people that will help you raise your children. Assembling a team comprised of skilled, compassionate people is the best strategy for surviving the delicate first three years following the death. Caring adults from schools, religious institutions, grief support centers, as well as therapists, family, tutors and friends can offer valuable support and insight. But everybody must agree that ultimately you are the Team Captain!

1. Get and keep the school involved – first and foremost alert your children's principal, teacher or counselor when the death occurs. Find out if the school has a plan for how to respond when a death impacts the school community. Check immediately with your children and find out if they would be comfortable if their classmates were informed about the death.

   With the advent of the internet, news travels quickly. Some children first find out about a death through a text message, tweet or on a facebook page. Make your family's preferences known, whether information will be disseminated to classmates and teachers or not. Younger children tend to like when they receive cards from classmates and when school personnel attend the funerary rituals. Your adolescent may feel uncomfortable if teachers or schools go out of their way to acknowledge their grief. Teens don't like being singled out and are likely to feel self-conscious if too much attention is given.

On the other hand, one teen expressed how hurt she felt when:

> *"The school made a big deal when another girl's parent died, but did nothing when my father died."*

In the event that your child has died, other children or teens can be offered the opportunity to grieve as a community and memorialize your child, their classmate, who died. Many schools will bring in grief counselors to provide onsite support when a student dies. Teachers might make a memorial bulletin board or hang banner paper so children can post a memory or a good-bye for their classmate. Parents report that they appreciate a strong show of support by the student body or staff when a child in the family has died.

School personnel can help other children understand how to support your grieving children. For example, another child can pick up assignments for your child prior to your child returning to school.

Identify who at the school can provide support for your children during the school day if they can't concentrate or experience a 'grief tsunami.' During quiet periods at school, thoughts or feelings related to the death may emerge. Grades may be impacted, either positively or negatively. Some kids report doing better because:

> *"That's what my dad would have wanted."*

Grades may also go down because there is no one at home to help them with homework, they aren't getting enough rest, good nutrition or can't focus in class. Encourage your school team member to keep you informed if there are academic, social or behavioral manifestations of the grief. Remember your children may not feel comfortable talking about their feelings or the death with classmates or adults at school. He or she may isolate, get teased, or even bullied when other students find out about the death.

Make sure that the teachers are aware when the death occurred and keep them informed about important dates or other events that might be impacting your children. Teachers may be unprepared to respond when a child is grieving. They may have unrealistic ideas about what is best for your children and might either lower their expectations or keep them unrealistically high. Help the school to understand your children's way of expressing their pain and make a plan including ways to support your children when their anger masks their pain. Give your children tools that will help them know how to respond when they are teased because they don't have a mom or dad, or when they distance themselves to avoid conflict. For example, teach them to walk away or seek support from an adult that they trust if they are mistreated during the school day.

You can also go outside the school community to recruit additional members of your team. Accept offers from friends and family who can help you with carpooling, picking up school assignments, driving to athletic practice or arranging play dates. Other mentors can be found at your religious organization, scout troop, or other extracurricular activities.

Recruit extended family when possible to fill some of the space left vacant after the death. Remember you can't be all things to all people. You are grieving too!

(See Chapter 10 for ways to determine if your child would benefit from individual or family therapy.)

CHAPTER 9:
HELP YOUR CHILDREN MAINTAIN THE CONNECTION AND MEMORIALIZE THEIR LOVED ONE

You may have grown up in a time or place where you heard that after a death it is better to "forget about it" and "move on." Some parentally-bereaved adults painfully recall coming home and finding that the clothing and personal belongings of their deceased parent had been removed without warning. Many were not even offered an opportunity to select an object which they could treasure and which would always remind them of their parent who had died. They recall the shock, sense of loss and anger that resulted from the removal of precious reminders of their loved one.

In some families there was a spoken or unspoken message not to ever mention the deceased person's name again for fear that the enormity of the loss would overtake them. Contrary to that style of grieving, most bereavement specialists now recognize the importance of maintaining the connection with the person who died. Your children will derive comfort from their happy memories which can be activated by mentioning the person who died by name and engaging in activities that memorialize or remind them of that person. For example, a trip to a favorite restaurant can be a pleasant time to remember the past and reconnect with positive feelings.

When your child experiences a 'grief tsunami' you can lead your child in a simple visualization exercise. Ask them to:

"Close your eyes and picture Mommy playing tag with you. Notice the smile on her face and the sound of her laughter.

Now open your eyes."

Typically children respond favorably after a simple visualization and experience comfort by reconnecting to the positive feelings they shared with their person who died.

Activities which help them maintain the bond also serve to remind the child that they had a parent (or sibling) who loved them. Consider the signal you send by removing or forbidding all reminders of the person who died. The pain of grief is not removed just because photos, belongings or conversation about the person has ceased. By helping your children hold on to their precious memories, you also teach them that each life matters and that we remember loved ones forever.

Share remembrances, photos, home movies and invoke the memory of the person who died by mentioning him or her in ordinary conversation. For example, on a trip to the ice cream store you notice your child ordering a flavor that was a favorite of the deceased. Casually mentioning:

"that was your brother's favorite flavor too"

will not only help them keep their memories alive, it will also signal that it's okay for them to mention the person who died.

Special days such as birthdays, the anniversary of the death and holidays can be challenging for grieving families. Prior to these special days, consider conducting a family meeting to discuss how you will remember your loved one. On the birthday of that person you may want to suggest having their favorite cake, going to their favorite restaurant, or doing something that person loved to do. Similarly, on the anniversary of the death you may decide to do these sorts of things, or light a candle, visit the cemetery or scattering site or engage in a memorial activity.

The absence of your loved one at holiday time can elicit strong emotions. A multitude of decisions must be faced including whether you will celebrate holidays with the traditions established before the death or create new rituals. Some families chose to 'take the year off' from their traditions knowing they can reinstate them when the family feels ready. Other families construct altars, hang their loved one's Christmas stocking, or make their favorite holiday dishes, toast the loved ones who have died, or even set a place for them at the holiday table.

Memorial activities such as the OUR HOUSE Run for Hope or a breast cancer walk/run, making a donation in your special person's honor, planting a tree, or building a memorial plaque are other ways family members can honor and memorialize throughout the year.

Many adults find that trips to the cemetery are the most logical ways to remember loved ones who have died. Your child may agree. However, never force your children to visit the gravesite if they do not want to and be prepared to offer to make other arrangements for them so that they don't have to go with you while you visit the cemetery. Inviting the children to accompany you and bring a painted rock, flowers, food or other decoration often makes the cemetery visit more upbeat. If they decline you may want to try inviting them again after some time has passed.

CHAPTER 10:
FREQUENTLY ASKED QUESTIONS

1. **Will my children survive this?**

   Yes. Children not only survive but thrive with your help and the help of your 'team.'

2. **How do I know if my children need therapy?**

   Children are extremely resilient following the death of a loved one. Joining a grief support group like those offered at OUR HOUSE both reduces the sense of isolation that many grieving children experience at school and may be enough outside support for your children. In some cases a grieving child or teen may experience more severe reactions and would benefit from psychotherapy by a grief specialist.

   As a rule, if your child is experiencing significant difficulty in two or more areas of their life, they may benefit from a short course of family or individual therapy. For example if their school work is fine but they are having difficulty at home and with peers, a psychotherapist specializing in working with grieving families might be a good addition to your team.

   In general, if your child or teen exhibits classic signs of depression including hopelessness, changes in their eating or sleeping habits, isolating from social interaction with peers, or if they express thoughts of harming themselves or troubled relations within the family, therapy might be indicated.

   In some cases your children might engage in high risk or erratic behavior because they can't express their grief any other way. A sudden and pronounced change in behavior would indicate greater psychological distress. For example running away from school to visit the cemetery because no one at school wants him around was a 9 year-old boys' cry for help.

Children as young as six may announce that they wish they were dead or that they want to kill themselves. One mother shared that her 7 year-old, outgoing, bon vivant son asked her if she ever thought about killing herself and reported that he:

"doesn't want to go on like this anymore."

She recognized that this was a cry for help and called for therapy referrals.

Caution: Expressing a wish to be dead doesn't always mean the child is thinking of ending his own life. Most children wish that they could be reunited with their person who died but have never considered hurting themselves or taking their own life.

Turning to drugs, alcohol or other self-destructive behaviors may be your children's way of attempting to ease the pain associated with grief. These behaviors impact your children's school performance and are potentially life threatening. Finding a therapist who specializes in substance abuse, cutting or other self-destructive behaviors would be advisable.

A grieving child may not feel like socializing or may need to stay close to you for comfort. If you are concerned that this behavior has gone on too long or your children start to express concern that their friends don't want to socialize with them, they may need professional help. In some circumstances children avoid a grieving child because the grieving child isn't *"as fun"* as other children. If this happens to your children you may encourage them to reach out and make plans with different, more compassionate playmates.

Since much of the adjustment that needs to happen after a death involves the entire family unit, family therapy may be helpful. That way you and your children can get professional assistance adjusting to the changes at home and learn new ways to communicate. At the same time, you can get the help you need establishing yourself as the head of the family.

3. Why is my child so afraid when we are apart?

After a loved one dies, your children will know that death happens and that it is unpredictable. They will be anxious and fearful that something may happen to you and you won't be able to care for them. Making and discussing an emergency plan which clearly outlines who would take care of your children if you were unable to care for them will alleviate some of their fears.

Make sure your children know how to contact you whenever you are apart. They need reassurance that you are there for them and being accessible by phone will give them a sense of control over the unpredictable environment. Their need to check in with you will decrease over time. Being consistent at pick up time after school, play dates or extracurricular activities is also very important.

While you can no longer say *"Don't worry, I'm not going to die,"* you can remind them of the ways you take good care of yourself and that you will most likely live a long life.

In addition, your child may be fearful that they might die when you are apart. Remind them that *"most people live until they are very, very old."*

If necessary, go with your child to the doctor and have the doctor offer reassurance that they aren't suffering from a life threatening illness.

Remember that both you and your children need to maintain your individuality, and that you can't be together all the time. Gradually your children will become more interested in engaging in activities on their own.

4. **What can I do to help my child through important life cycle events?**

   Before and after major events like birthdays, SAT tests, sporting events, performances, etc., children can learn to do a simple visualization exercise. Encourage them to try and visualize the face and words of encouragement that their parent or sibling would have offered if that person were still alive. By picturing their face or voice at these special times they re-experience that pleasurable sensation of support they once received and enjoyed from their loved one who died.

5. **What are some ways I can help my children maintain a connection with their loved one?**

   By helping your children retain the memory of the sound of the person's voice or laughter and what they looked like, you will ease their pain during the initial period of mourning. Slowly over time those images may fade. This may be experienced as another loss. Explain that it is normal to forget over time but that, if possible, they can look at photos, recordings or home movies to refresh their memories.

Family projects such as memory books, photos albums, and memory boxes aid in this process. Some people like to make quilts or pillow cases composed of squares cut from t-shirts, ties, or blouses that belonged to the person who died.

Planting a tree, painting a rock or hanging a memorial plaque in a garden or other cherished spot offer children the chance to have a place they can go to remember, in addition to visiting a cemetery or scattering site.

CHAPTER 11:
HELPING YOUR CHILD COPE WITH YOUR NEW RELATIONSHIP

While it may be hard now to imagine dating after the death of a spouse or life partner you may, at some point, find yourself ready. Remarriage or re-partnering may have a positive impact not only on you but also on your children. Grief experts have found that if you marry after a "suitable period of time," and it's someone who your children enjoy, it will bring more resources into the household and positively impact the outcome of the child's mourning process.

Consider the following when you feel ready to start dating:

1. Ask yourself whether your absence from the home while dating will have a negative impact on the children. This can add to their feelings of abandonment.

2. It will be easier on your children if you only date someone who feels comfortable when your partner who died is mentioned.

3. When you date someone who is also a parent, your children may feel threatened or abandoned because they now have to share you with another family. The presence of this other family creates a competition for your affections.

4. Your children will also worry that you will forget their parent who died or that you didn't love him or her.

5. Understand that even though you may feel ready to date, your children might not be ready.

6. Serial dating may introduce additional losses into the life of your children. Consider waiting to introduce the person until you are exclusive with your new partner.

Once you embark upon your new relationship:

1. The first contacts with your children should be brief such as a meal out at a restaurant rather than a dinner at home.

2. Refrain from overnights in your home as long as possible. In addition, children report great distress when they know that their surviving parent is 'sneaking out' for an 'overnight' after they are supposed to be asleep. If you plan to go out for an overnight, let your children know who will care for them and how they can contact you if needed.

3. Make time to spend with your children without your new partner being present. This will help ease the pain of having to share you with someone else.

4. Make sure that you show them that you have not forgotten the person who died but that you have plenty of love to share.

CHAPTER 12:
THERE'S NO SUCH THING AS CLOSURE!

In our goal-oriented society, people are led to believe that if they complete the 'stages of grief' they will achieve closure. However, grief is not a disease for which there is a cure. What you can expect to happen is that the intensity of the grief will lessen and painful memories will grow fewer. Over time, you and your children will become more fully engaged in the present and, eventually, more future-oriented. While you and your children will never be the same as you were before the death, you can go on in the absence of the person who died and grow as a result of the experience.

As your children enter new developmental stages their grief reactions are likely to change. Grief, like true love, does not ever go away but is always with you. Life cycle events such as weddings, communions, graduations etc. are likely to trigger new waves of grief and challenges. Normalize that this is an expected part of the healing process. For example, when your son or daughter prepares to marry they may wonder who will walk them down the aisle. If you and your family experience considerable distress you might want to consider returning briefly to family or individual therapy to help you and the family cope with these challenges.

Always remember that children and teens are resilient and that if they receive grief support from their families and their community, they can live happy and productive lives. You will realize one day that not only are your children surviving, but that they are thriving!

At OUR HOUSE, we hold the hope for the future for the participants in our grief support groups. We encourage you to hold onto that hope as you make your way through your grief journey towards healing.

Children Grieve Too:
a handbook for parents of grieving children and teens

About the author:

Lauren Schneider, LCSW

Clinical Director of Child and Adolescent Programs, OUR HOUSE Grief Support Center

Lauren, a nationally recognized authority on Children's Grief, has provided training for mental health clinicians, educators and graduate students throughout the community since 2000. She created "My Memory Book… for grieving children" as well as curriculum for use at Camp Erin Los Angeles and in OUR HOUSE grief support groups. She trains and supervises OUR HOUSE group leaders as well as MSW and MFT clinicians and students. Lauren leads in-house and school-based grief support groups and maintains a private practice.